Pearl

"The Dreamer and His Pearl"
(from the original fourteenth-century manuscript illustration)

PEARL

Translated from the Middle English poem
by the anonymous author of
Sir Gawain and the Green Knight,
fourteenth century,
from the Cotton Nero A.x manuscript book
in the British Library

A NEW VERSE TRANSLATION IN MODERN ENGLISH

WITH A PREFACE BY

John Ridland

AND AN INTRODUCTION BY
Maryann Corbett

ABLE MUSE PRESS

First published in 2018 by

Able Muse Press

www.ablemusepress.com

Printed in the United States of America

Library of Congress Control Number: 2017930323

ISBN 978-1-927409-88-6 (paperback)
ISBN 978-1-77349-026-7 (hardcover)
ISBN 978-1-927409-89-3 (digital)

Introduction by Maryann Corbett

Cover image & frontispiece: Illustration from the original manuscript in the British Library, Cotton Nero A.x

Cover & book design by Alexander Pepple

Able Muse Press is an imprint of *Able Muse:* A Review of Poetry, Prose & Art—at
www.ablemuse.com

Able Muse Press
467 Saratoga Avenue #602
San Jose, CA 95129

Setting a Jewel:

An Introduction to the Historical Background of Pearl

*D*AZZLING: IT'S THE SINGLE WORD fixed firmly in my mind as a characterization of the Middle English *Pearl*. The poem and the word have been linked in my head ever since a fellow student pulled an adjective out of the glittering party-conversation air in my graduate school days. The word fits because the poem is a marvel: structurally complete and complex in mathematical design; multiple in its symmetries as a faceted gem; never flagging in the sonic satisfactions of its meter and rhyme; and compelling narratively, emotionally, and—for the right readers—in the turns and twists of its arguments.

It is not at all surprising that John Ridland, after having translated *Sir Gawain and the Green Knight*, would decide to translate another work by (as scholars generally agree) the same poet. Having grappled with *Gawain*'s Northwest Midland dialect, he wanted, I'm sure, to put that experience to further use. As I wrote in my foreword to *Gawain*, that poem manifestly needed a translator willing to use a novel approach to its meter, namely the heptameter or ballad meter that Ridland uses. Heptameter leaves the translator enough room in each line for all of that poem's extravagant and very long-lined detail.

Pearl shares every bit of that extravagance, but its meter is quite different. It fits its flashiness into lines that the modern ear understands as accentual tetrameter, and it adds to that the most intricate rhyme scheme of its day. The challenge for the translator is to convey all the aspects of this dazzle in an English that stays contemporary and unstrained. That means finding terms in modern English that maintain the intricate ballade-like rhyme scheme without distorting the meanings of Northwest Midland words that have no heirs in present-day speech. That's a puzzle with all the fascination of the Rubik's cube and the Sudoku book. The fairly tight meter is another puzzle piece, backing translators into corners of archaism and awkwardness. The problems of rhyme, meter, alliteration, and repetition combined explain why new renderings of *Pearl* are always appearing, with poets constantly disagreeing about which of the original elements can or should be maintained.[1]

In his preface, Ridland explains the complexities of handling that rhyme scheme, the shortcomings of other translators' attempts, and his choice of the Shakespearean sonnet pattern as a compromise. I approve of his choice, because the sonnet has affinities to French and Italian fourteenth-century poems that were gaining influence in the late fourteenth century, just as the *Pearl*'s stanza form does. I also approve of it because it gives all the satisfying chimes of a rhyme scheme without the usual straining of idiom. Such a compromise is just one of the many weighings and balancings that translation demands.

For *Pearl* there are challenges of translation beyond these. As the editors of *Modern Poetry in Translation* say on the magazine's web site, "The past is a foreign country as much as anywhere else beyond our frontiers now." Both the immediate world of the poet and the larger England of the fourteenth century are more foreign than we probably realize.

---

1. For a recent list of the many translations, see https://medievalpearl.wordpress.com/pearls-editionstranslations/.

The first foreignness is that we cannot say for certain who the poet is or what audience he had in mind. Nothing written in the poem tells us explicitly where it comes from; no author or scribe is named. The poem survives in a single copy, along with three other poems, in a small manuscript that can be dated to the late fourteenth century and assigned by linguistic research to the Northwest Midlands, most probably Cheshire. Between the time of its creation and the seventeenth century, the book's whereabouts are unknown; we have no idea who owned it, or why. It turns up in Yorkshire in "a list of manuscripts made before 1614," and in 1621 it was cataloged in the library of Sir Robert Cotton. (Cotton's system of identifying bookcases with busts of Roman emperors, and lettering and numbering their shelves, is the source of the name we still give to that book—Cotton Nero A.x—as well as one of the names of the famous manuscript that preserves *Beowulf,* Cotton Vitellius A.xv.) After surviving that library's 1731 fire, it was moved to the British Library in 1753. It received little attention until the nineteenth century, when Sir Frederick Madden translated one of its four poems, now the best known, *Sir Gawain and the Green Knight.*

So the poem's origin and its early history have gone unrecorded. We have no clear information about who the poet was, or why he wrote. Without knowing those things, we cannot be entirely sure what he means by what he says— which ideas in the air of his time he is supporting, which he is contradicting.

On its glittering surface, the poem looks straightforward and appealing. Its emotions seem authentically like those of a father who has lost his young child. It is cast in the common medieval form of a dream vision, in which a person troubled by grief or confusion converses in a dream with someone who guides him to peace of mind, and it is also cast as an allegory, in which a being described as a pearl clearly represents something, or someone, other. It takes materials that are well known to its audience—the matter of Christian theology and scripture, visual symbolism, and the language of courtly love—and weaves them into something new, in an intricate and pleasing structure.

But in doing so, it betrays almost nothing about its author. This is not typical of poets of the time; Chaucer, Gower, and Langland all gave us information about themselves; so did contemporary French poets like Christine de Pizan. Charles Muscatine has noted that in all four poems collected in Cotton Nero A.x, the author is evasive about the details of his life to a degree that seems like a form of escapism, a retreat from life (37, 40). Was it merely that? Was he vague for a reason? What sort of person wrote *Pearl?* While it is fruitless to try to assign *Pearl* to a specific author (though a number of scholars have tried), I think it is fruitful for the readers of this translation to think about what status the poet may have held and what ideas were swirling around him.

Modern readers will probably prefer to see the poem as autobiographical. It is reasonable and emotionally compelling to assume that the poet *is* his narrator, the Dreamer, and that he actually is the bereaved father of a dead two-year-old daughter. Critics have taken many other positions, though. The conclusion that "the pearl" is the Dreamer's infant daughter is based on only two clear statements of his: that she is "nearer to me than aunt or niece" and that she was with him for less than two years. A number of interpreters have gone in other directions. For some the pearl is a symbol of virginity. Others have seen the poem as an allegory of the progress of the Dreamer's own soul. For a useful and up-to-date rundown of the scholarship, see the introduction to Sarah Stanbury's edition of the poem, available both in print and online.

But even scholars who accept that the poem is an elegy and the pearl a child sometimes argue that the author and the bereaved narrator might not be the same person. The way texts were produced in fourteenth-century England, within a patronage system, makes it much more likely (they contend) that the poem was a commissioned work. Perhaps it was written to mark an anniversary of a death, probably a death of the daughter of a noble family (Stanbury 10–11). The grieving father could have been the poet's patron, much in the same way that John of Gaunt was the patron who commissioned Chaucer's *Book of the Duchess* to honor Blanche, Gaunt's late wife.

This is an image of the poet, the occasion, and the audience that I find believable. (For fuller arguments and citations, see the introductions to the Stanbury and Vantuono editions, cited below.) This picture fits, too, with the notion that the same poet wrote *Gawain* and *Pearl,* as well as the manuscript's other poems, *Cleanness* and *Patience.* The high polish and intricate design of *Pearl,* its use of the material of courtly love as well as of learned theology, and its extravagant descriptions of costly objects all suggest that it was made by and for people of wealth and status, not only the patron himself but the aristocratic set in which he moved. The poem succeeds as elegy, but it is elegy as art object. It is, it seems to me, a court-oriented poem, just as *Gawain* is.

But there is a problem here: none of the court-oriented poems in Cotton Nero A.x found a continuing fan base among the English court's readers and book collectors. The book was not copied and recopied, as popular fourteenth-century books commonly were. The poems apparently lost their audience and disappeared for centuries. If they had the support of a patron, especially a court patron, what accounts for that disappearance? The work of John M. Bowers suggests some answers, and I summarize them here. Bowers operates on the theory that the Dreamer and the poet are one and the same, and he explains what sort of person that was, what his circumstances were, and what ideas concerned him.

Much depends on the notion that the *Pearl* poet was connected to the court of Richard II. The manuscript and its language can be dated to the time of his reign, and it is known that Richard had close connections to Cheshire, involving a large number of Cheshiremen in the workings of his household and his private army. So we need first to imagine that the poet was close to that court, and not in a regional outpost in Cheshire, but in London. To get a quick image of the opulence of the court, and of Richard's idea of the absolute and sacred role of a king—and to be reminded of his sad end—the reader cannot do better than to watch an online production of Shakespeare's *Richard II.*

What was the nature of the poet's connection to the court? *Pearl* makes clear that its author had a clerical education: he spends many lines in theological argument and is familiar with scripture and patristics. We can reasonably picture him as a cleric of some kind. Holy orders were a requirement for many administrative positions, so he probably held a post of that type. And his clerical status may be the reason he says so little about his relationship to the dead child. If he was a subdeacon, deacon, or priest, it would have been scandalous for him to have fathered a child, although there is plenty of evidence that such scandals were frequent. Of course, he may have been in one of the minor orders, those below subdeacon, and so allowed to marry. But clerics who remained in minor orders to preserve their right to marry were often criticized for doing so. So, that too might explain the *Pearl* poet's reticence about having a daughter.

But clerical status alone does not explain why he spends so much time on certain points of catechism and scripture. That baptism effectively washes away all sin is a standard point of Christian thinking; why does the poet elaborate it for ten stanzas? The parable of the workers in the vineyard (Matthew 20:1–16) is also a commonplace, yet the poem draws out the standard interpretation for another tenth of its length. Why?

One clue is the swirling social unrest caused by the views of the Lollards, the followers of the heretic John Wycliff. (Readers who recall their Chaucer may remember that the Host accuses the Parson of being one of these.) Lollardy unsettled not only the church but the entire social order, from the king down, particularly after John Ball, the leader of the Peasants' Revolt, had preached its heretical tenets. In the latter part of Richard's reign, Lollard opinions were spreading widely, and the same court that had tolerated them early on was now taking strenuous measures to oppose them.

What were the Lollards saying about baptism that might have moved the *Pearl* poet? Some were arguing that infant baptism was void since the child could not consent, others that it was needless if both parents were baptized, and still others that a bastard child could not in any case be saved. The air was roiling with unorthodox opinions, and the *Pearl* poet, voicing the conservative position of the court, and probably his own theology and his own feelings, would have been intent on opposing them. He even allows his Dreamer to ask dull-witted questions so that he can lay out his arguments in full.

His court-centered outlook also explains the many lines he spends on the Parable of the Vineyard. He is doing more than justifying a full heavenly reward for a child; he is also siding with the king and the aristocracy and against the march of economic history in the most pressing class dispute of the time: laborers against landowners. The Black Death had greatly reduced the number of peasants available to work the land, and peasants who realized how badly landowners needed them had begun to bargain with their lords for better terms. Some even left the lands they were bound to and looked to different masters for pay that was higher, and in cash. Landowners needing to get their crops harvested had little recourse but to hire for a short term and increased pay, even though they complained bitterly, and Parliament tried time and again to legislate against the practice. When the *Pearl* poet stresses the right of the lord to pay exactly what he chooses, without regard to what the workers think is fair, and when he stresses the covenanted rate, he is alluding pointedly to a political argument, not just a theological one.

Finally, why did this poet's work pass out of memory? The reputations of other poets connected with Richard's court, like Chaucer and Gower, only continued to grow, in spite of Richard's fate, and West Midland dialect did not interfere with the popularity of *Piers Plowman*. The most reasonable explanation is that on Richard's deposition and death, the Cheshire contingent that had enjoyed his preferment was cut off by his successor, Henry IV. It is known that at his accession Henry failed to renew the annuities of most of Richard's Cheshiremen. That could well have meant the end of support for the *Pearl* poet, and for his local patron if he had one, as well as the end of the opulence and generous patronage of art that Richard had favored.

This particular past—as I have laid it out, following Bowers— is indeed a foreign country. I hope that by translating that past for John Ridland's readers I have made it easier to enjoy *Pearl's* dazzling surface, to appreciate its narrative and emotional heft, and to see a little beneath all that, to the complicated mind that set such a jewel.

Maryann Corbett

★ ★ ★

Works Consulted

Bowers, John M. *The Politics of Pearl: Court Poetry in the Age of Richard II.* Cambridge: D.S. Brewer, 2001.

Muscatine, Charles. "The *Pearl* Poet: Style as Defense." In *Poetry and Crisis in the Age of Chaucer.* Notre Dame: University of Notre Dame Press, 1972. Pp. 37–69.

Pearl, ed. Sarah Stanbury. Kalamazoo, Michigan: Medieval Institute Publications, 2001. Also http://d.lib.rochester.edu/teams/text/stanbury-pearl

Pearl: An Edition with Verse Translation. Trans. William Vantuono. Notre Dame: University of Notre Dame Press, 1995.

Translator's Preface

GAWAIN IS RIGHTLY CLASSIFIED AS an Arthurian Romance, and *Pearl* as a dream vision elegy, like Chaucer's early poem, "The Book of the Duchess." The difference from Chaucer is that the narrator of *Pearl* says he is mourning the death of his own little girl, less than two years old, while Chaucer is writing on commission for his patron John of Gaunt, Duke of Lancaster, whose wife Blanche had died. *The Book of the Duchess* is spoken by a third person who observes the grief of the widowed "Man in Black," but the narrator of *Pearl* speaks as the grieving father himself. However fanciful and conventional some aspects of the vision may be, and thus less likely to have been elements of a real dream, the speaker's emotions feel quite authentic, and in thinking about the poem, a reader should not be discouraged from considering it, as many scholars have done, as based on the poet's experience of losing a young child.

Turning to the form of the poem, it is mathematically ordered as well as verbally. There are 101 stanzas, exactly the same number as in *Sir Gawain and the Green Knight,* a coincidence which is taken as evidence that the same person wrote both poems, since there weren't any others around at that time with that number. (Which was written first is uncertain.) Trying to decide a question of authorship with such slender evidence, however, is fruitless. It seems best to accept that the probabilities are high these two masterpieces were written by the one unknown poet. (Incidentally, none of the titles the four poems are known by appears in the manuscript.)

The Roman numeral part numbers are traditionally provided by editors to mark the "quintets" of stanzas with similarly worded last lines (and the single exception, number XV, with six stanzas). I have followed other translators in assigning Arabic numerals to each stanza for ease of reference.

More than with most of the translations I have made, I have had to accept, in *Pearl*, a limitation that I am loath to adopt, by not replicating the rhyme scheme exactly. The original is described by Maryann Corbett as "the most intricate of its age." Laid out in the usual alphabetical scheme, its twelve lines rhyme like a babbling brook: *abababababbcbc*. Thus, in the original the first stanza reads:

> Perle, pleasaunt to princes *pay*
> To clanly close in gold so *clere–*
> Out of orient, I hardily *say,*
> Ne proved I never her precious *pere:*
> 5 So rounde, so reken in uch *aray,*
> So small, so smothe her sides *were,*
> Wheresoever I jugged gemmes *gay,*
> I set her sengeley in *synglere.*
> Alas, I lest her in an *erbere:*
> 10 Thurgh gresse to grounde hit fro me *yot.*
> I dewyne, fordolked of luf-*daungere*
> Of that privy perle withouten *spot.*

(Incidentally, though this was not my purpose, this stanza like almost every other answers the question of why the poem needs to be translated for a general reader of modern English, if not for a graduate student.)

A literal prose translation, missing some of the wordplay, [and with some explanatory extensions in brackets] could read:[2]

---

2. I have followed the spelling of the recent Penguin Classics edition of *The Works of the Gawain Poet,* edited by Ad Putter and Myra Stokes (Penguin Books, 2014).

Pearl, pleasant for a prince's pleasure to enclose cleanly in bright gold—I boldly assert that I never met with [or *assayed*, as a jeweler would do] her peer in value even among Oriental pearls [which were the most valued]: so round, so splendid in any setting, so small, so smooth were her sides [scholars note that the same terms were used by the male poets in romantic love poetry to describe the women] that wherever I judged beautiful gems, I set her apart, alone in her singularity. Alas, I lost her in a (herb) garden: she went (fell) from me through the grass into the earth. I languish, badly wounded by my frustrated separation in love [again, this sounds like a romantic lover's talk] for that hidden spotless pearl.

Poetry is most assuredly what is lost in translation when the translator merely turns it into prose like this. The notorious difficulty of rhyming in modern English is brought into relief by the comparative ease of Middle English. Professor Marie Boroff deserves an ovation for her truly valiant attempt to follow the rhyme scheme all the way, as she declares:

> I have reproduced the schemes of rhyme, repetition, and concatenation . . . : whatever difficulties these present, the poem could scarcely retain its identity without them.[3]

The language in her translation of this stanza form is more natural than not—an extraordinary accomplishment, but even she is forced by the end-rhyming pattern into syntactical distortions, anachronisms, and inversions of word order that don't sound quite like good contemporary English, for instance, those underlined in the first stanza:

---

3. *Sir Gawain and the Green Knight, Patience, and Pearl: Verse Translations* by Marie Boroff (W. W. Norton, New York and London, 2001). Ms. Borroff also footnotes every reference to the Bible, of which the poem makes well over one hundred, and helpfully reprints (on pages 163–165) the most relevant passages from Apocalypse or the Book of Revelations.

Pearl, that a prince is well content
To give a circle of gold to wear,
Boldly I say, all orient
Brought forth none precious like to her;
5   So comely every ornament,
So slender her sides, so smooth they were,
Ever my mind was bound and bent
To set her apart without a peer.
In a garden of herbs I lost my dear;
10   Through grass to ground away it shot;
Now, lovesick, the heavy loss I bear
Of that secret pearl without a spot.

Simon Armitage takes the road most traveled by contemporary translators, intending

> to allow rhymes to occur as naturally as possible within sentences, internally or at the end of lines, and to let half-rhymes and syllabic [?] rhymes play their part, and for the poem's musical orchestration to be performed by pronounced alliteration, looping repetition, and the quartet of beats in each line. So formalists and technicians scanning for a ladder of rhyme words down the right-hand margin of this translation will be frustrated, though hopefully my solution will appeal to the ear and the voice.[4]

So his first stanza reads:

> Beautiful pearl that would please a prince,
> fit to be mounted in finest gold,
> I say for certain that in all the East
> her precious equal I never found.

---

4. *Pearl: A New Verse Translation* by Simon Armitage (Liveright, New York and London, 2016).

5   So radiant and round, however revealed,
        so small, her skin so very smooth,
        of all the gems I judged and prized
        I set her apart, unparalleled.
        But I lost my pearl in a garden of herbs;
10   she slipped from me through grass to ground,
        and I mourn now, with a broken heart
        for that priceless pearl without a spot.

Lacking the "ladder of rhymes," however, it is only the approximation of meter that enables a translation to climb above the ground level of a prose paraphrase.

My own version is a more restrictive approximation of the original, maintaining its loose iambic/anapestic tetrameter and its rhyme, though not reproducing the four-fold repetitious pattern of the original. The manuscript is unpunctuated, and therefore the editors of the text must choose where to put the commas, periods, colons, and semicolons. After I noticed that most of those twelve-line stanzas divide syntactically into three quatrains, as the punctuation of texts and translations by various editors shows, it struck me that a compromise between rigid fidelity and casual infidelity could be found in the familiar rhyme scheme of a Shakespearean sonnet, the old reliable *abab cdcd efef.* As for the rhyming itself, I have been laxer than in some previous translations (for example, the Hungarian Sándor Petöfi's *John the Valiant*). When I could find no true rhyme that wouldn't sound merely clever, I let the sounds go slant. This is not an excuse for laziness but a reluctant admission that modern English word order makes end-rhyming harder than the syntactical flexibility of Middle English. Further, wherever the original wording could be carried over into modern English without losing its meaning, which is surprisingly often, I have done that. And in my final revision I relied heavily on the Penguin Classics edition of *The Works of the* Gawain *Poet,* already noted, which means that many of the phrasings are identical with theirs, except for the rhyme and meter into which I have poured them.

Thus my first stanza reads:

> Pearl that would please a prince's eyes
> In a bright gold setting, radiant,
> I never met such a precious prize
> Among all those out of the Orient.
> 5   So round, so bright in any display,
> So smooth, so slender her sides, in my mind,
> Wherever I judge fair gems, I say,
> I set her off as one of a kind.
> In a garden of herbs I lost her and mourn.
> 10   She dropped from me through the grass to that plot.
> By Love's power I'm stricken and grief-torn
> For my hidden pearl without a spot.

I will leave it to readers to compare these versions minutely if they wish, but let me note what I thought the poem needed: the feeling of continuous forward movement, of momentum, that meter in its nature provides, and with the places in that movement where one can pause for breath signaled by the end rhymes. And these are marked more quietly, I would argue, by not following the virtuoso juggling of three rhymes per stanza in the original: only two for lines 1–10 and 11, and the third interrupting at 10 and closing the stanza off at 12, a little like the Shakespearean couplet.

The *Pearl* poet outdoes all of us, not only in the relative ease with which he persists in that elaborate scheme, but in the extras he throws in, like an Olympic platform diver adding a couple of twists to a three-and-a-half somersault. Every five stanzas carry something like a refrain line linking them together as a group. I can picture the poet, once he had set himself this pattern, keeping it in mind as he climbed down the ladder of his rhyme scheme, adjusting the meaning so that it fits the form. When the first of five stanzas has ended, for example in line 12:

> Of that privy perle withouten spot.

he leads into something very close to it (and in some groups often identical) at the ends of the next four stanzas:

> My privy perle withouten spot. (24)
> Of that precious perle withouten spot. (36)
> My precious perle withouten spot. (48)
> On that precious perle withouten spot. (60)

And then, as if thinking, *That was too easy,* he tosses a key word from the first stanza's concatenation up into the first line of the next stanza, though with less exact repetition (in this case, as in many, by punning: *spot* moves from its sense of "stain" to its other meaning of "a particular place"):

> Syn in that *spot* hit fro me sprang, (13)
> That *spot* of spices mot nedes sprede, (25)
> To that *spot* that I in speche expound (37)
> Before that *spot* my hande I spenned (49)

And finally (massive spoiler alert!), the last line of the whole poem circles around to echo the first, as the wording shifts from

> Perle, plesaunt to princes pay (1)

to

> And precious perles unto His pay. (1212)

The capital letter on "His" (in three of the six editions I have consulted) has transformed the ordinary, jewel-collecting, secular prince of line one into the Prince of the New Jerusalem Himself, to whom the Dreamer's Pearl (along with 143,999 other virgins) is married. But that is getting ahead of the story, which begins with a narrator, a man, in the green herbal garden where the pearl he dropped on the grass has been buried in the ground—a simple allegory for the death and burial of his two-year-old daughter. And so the elegy begins.

John Ridland

Contents

PEARL

I

1.

Pearl that would please a prince's eyes
In a bright gold setting, radiant,
I never met such a precious prize
Among all those out of the Orient.
So round, so right in any display,
So smooth, so slender her sides, in my mind,
Wherever I judge fair gems, I say,
I set her off as one of a kind.
In a garden of herbs I lost her and mourn.
10   She dropped from me through the grass to that plot.
By Love's loss I'm stricken and grief-torn
For my hidden pearl without a spot.

2.

Since in that spot it sprang from me,
I've often watched, and wished for its wealth,
That used to keep me sorrow-free
And raise my spirits and mend my health;
It wrings my heart with such great force
My breast both swells and seethes with grief,
Yet I thought I'd never, from any source,
20   Heard song so sweet steal to my relief,
And many hushed songs have stolen my way.
To think of her color so clad in a clod!
You spoil a splendid jewel in your clay,
Oh earth, my own pearl without a spot.

3.

That spot of spice is bound to spread
Where such rich rotting has begun.
Blossoms of white and blue and red
Shine sheerly bright beneath the sun.
Flower and fruit won't be denied
30   Where the pearl drove down into that dark loam.
For each plant sprouts from seeds that have died
Or wheat won't flourish for harvest home.
Each good begins from another good thing;
Such a lovely seed fulfills its lot
So the burgeoning spices too should spring
From that precious pearl without a spot.

4.

In that spot I speak of, as you may hear,
I entered into the herbal green,
In August at that high time of year
40   When corn is cut with scythes made keen.
Where the pearl had gone rolling down the mound,
These bright and beautiful plants cast shadows.
There gillyflower, ginger, and gromwell abound,
And peonies powdered as in a meadow.
If it was beautiful to perceive,
Yet a fairer fragrance came floating out.
For there that priceless one lives, I believe,
My precious pearl without a spot.

5.

In front of that spot I clenched my fingers

50   At the bitter sorrow in which I was caught.

Deep in my heart a dulled grief lingers:

Though Reason attempted to settle my thought.

I mourned my pearl so tightly bound,

Put forth fierce, forceful arguments; though

The nature of Christ could bring me around,

My wretched will worked me up into woe.

I fell down on that flowery grass.

And through my brain such fragrance shot,

To a sudden fit of sleep I passed

60   On that precious pearl without a spot.

II

6.[5]

With that, my spirit sprang from that spot;
My body lay dreaming on the mound.
My soul had soared, by the grace of God,
Questing where marvels could be found.
I'd no idea where I was—what place,
But I knew I'd been cast where cliffs clove the sky.
Toward a forest I turned my face,
Where resplendent rocks I could descry.
None would believe the light they shed,
70   Their gleaming, glorious radiance,
For never, in tapestries men have made,
Were half such splendid ornaments.

---

5. The Dream begins here and is not broken until line 1170.

7.

All of the hillsides were decorated
With clear crystal cliffs in a natural show.
The bright woods all around them waited,
Their trunks as blue as indigo.
Like burnished silver, leaves sliding over
Leaves, dense on each branch, were quivering;
When the cloud-free gleams went gliding over,
80   Their sheen shone shrilly,[6] shivering.
The gravel crunching underfoot
Was precious pearls from the Orient.
Sunbeams are dusky, dark as soot,
By contrast with that ornament.

---

6. Putter and Stokes note this as the first "inspired transcendence" (or "synesthesia") in English until Tennyson (Notes, 411).

8.

The ornaments of the much-loved hill
Led my soul to forget its grief.
Such fragrance from the fruit trees spilled,
Like delicious food to my relief.
The birds flew through the woods, arrayed
90   In flaming hues, both small and great;
Citole string and gitternist played,
And their splendid music would not abate;
For while the birds were beating their wings,
They sang in harmonious sweet assent.
There is no one who more sweetly sings
Than you hear and see in their ornaments.

9.

So all was adorned in such splendid style
In that forest Fortune was leading me to,
That describing its glory would be futile—
100   What no speaker, however fluent, could do.
I walked on, always in blissful awe;
No bank loomed dangerous in the air.
The farther I went, the fairer I saw:
The meadow, the bushes, the spice, the pears,
And hedge-rows, and water-meadows, and more—
Its steep sides glowed like fine gold thread.
I came to a stream's sheer sloping shore:
What splendid ornaments, Lord, were spread!

10.

　　　The ornaments of those splendid depths
110　Were banks of clear bright beryl stone;
　　　Swirling sweetly, the water swept
　　　With a whispering sound flowing on and on.
　　　Gems covered the bottom, brilliant and bright,
　　　And glinted and glowed like light through glass,
　　　Or stars in the heavens on a winter night,
　　　While countryfolk sleep, and the light-streams pass;
　　　For every pebble that lay in the pool
　　　Matched emerald or sapphire in elegance,
　　　Thus the water gleamed with light like jewels,
120　So splendid were its ornaments.

III

11.

On hill and dale such splendor waited,
Of beautiful plains, and water and woods,
It built up my bliss, my pains abated,
Dispelled my distress, my losses made good.
Down by the stream that's always flowing
I wandered in bliss. Joy brimmed in my brain
In these watery valleys. The more I kept going,
The stronger the joy my mind could contain.
For whenever Fortune makes trial of a man,
130   Sending him solace, or pressing him sore,
That one whom she tests, as only she can,
Of good or of ill, shall have more and more.

12.

Thus more good fortune came in this wise
Than I could relate if I had the leisure,
But an earthly heart could never suffice
For a tenth part of that joyful pleasure.
Therefore I thought that Paradise
Was over those broad banks, and the breaks
In the water pools I supposed a device
140   To plant pleasure gardens among the lakes.
Beyond the brook, past slope or glade,
I hoped to see a walled castle soar,
But the water was deep; I dared not wade,
However I longed to, more and more.

13.

More and more, and yet even more,
I longed to look beyond that stream,
For though it was fair on the nearer shore,
Much lovelier did the farther seem.
I stopped and, all around, I stared;
150   I looked for a ford where I might stand,
But there were more dangers to be dared
The farther I stalked along the strand,
And always I thought I should not change
My course from fear, such joys to explore.
Then I noted something new and strange
That troubled my thinking more and more.

14.

A greater marvel subdued my sense:
I saw beyond that sparkling run
A crystal cliff stood in full resplendence;
160   Royal rays rose from it to the sun.
A young girl sat at the foot of it—quite
A gentle maiden, of courteous air;
Her mantle was a gleaming white.
I knew her well, I'd seen her elsewhere.
Like gleaming gold sliced to threads of hair,
That fair one shone from across the shore.
For a long time I looked upon her there:
The longer, I knew her more and more.

15.

The more I studied her lovely face,
170   And the fine figure into which she had grown,
Such gladdening glory lit up that space
Of a sort which I had seldom known.
I wanted to call her, but, to begin,
Bewilderment gave my heart a jolt.
So strange was the place I saw her in
That a shout might stab my heart like a bolt.
And then she lifted her beautiful brow,
The ivory-white visage that she wore.
My heart stood stunned in confusion now,
180   And ever the longer, more and more.

IV

16.

More than I wished, my dread arose;
I stood stock-still and dared not call;
With eyes wide open and mouth tight closed,
I stood like a hooded hawk in a hall.
I trusted the spirit was spiritual;
I was afraid of what might occur
If she escaped me beyond recall
Before I could stop her and talk to her.
That gracious, beautiful, spotless girl,
190   So smooth, so slender, so finely bound,
Arose in royal array, a pearl,
A precious being in pearl surround.

17.

Set among pearls of royal price,
There might a man with good luck hope
To see, when, fresh as a *fleur-de-lys,*
The maid came straightway down the slope.
Her surcoat and fine mantle gleamed,
With open sides, and its borders shone
With the prettiest pearls, or so it seemed,
200   That I had ever set eyes upon,
With wide flowing sleeves, I could clearly see,
Where double rows of pearls abounded;
Her bright skirt matched it perfectly,
With precious pearls set all around it.

18.

Set around the crown that was that girl's
Were only pearls, no other stone,
High-pinnacled with pure white pearls
As perfect flowers around each one;
No other circlet crowned the girl.
210   It framed her face all on its own,
And solemn enough for duke or earl,
Her hue was whiter than whale's bone.
Her hair, like shorn gold, lay athwart
Her shoulders, shining in disorder.
Her own rich color did not fall short
Of the luster of pearls in her garment's border.

19.

Adorned was her wristband, and every hem—
At her hands, her sides, the neck opening—
With white pearls and no other gem,
220 And radiant white was all her clothing.
But a wondrous, flawless pearl, a treasure,
In the midst of her breast was set firm and trim:
Before one's mind could take its measure,
His power to judge might abandon him.
I think no tongue could have the power
To comprehend that marvelous sight,
It was so clean and bright and pure,
That precious pearl, where it was set.

20.

Adorned in pearls, that precious sweet

230   Came down the opposite slope to the stream.

No man from here to Greece you'd meet

Was gladder than I when she stood on the brim;

She was nearer to me than aunt or niece:

My joy was therefore all the more.

She offered to speak, that special spice,

Bowing womanly low beside the shore:

She cast off her crown, her greatest treasure,

And hailed me with a joyful cry.

I was glad I'd been born to know this pleasure,

240   To that sweet adorned in pearls, to reply!

V

21.

"O Pearl," I said, "whom pearls adorn,
Are you my pearl for whom I've burned
And grieved, alone from night till morn?
I have concealed how much I've yearned
Since you slid from me into the soil,
Impaired and saddened and afflicted,
While you live leisurely, without toil,
In Paradise, quite unconflicted.
What Fate has ripped my jewel from my heart?
250   What separation could be crueler?
Since we like twins were torn apart,
I have become a joyless jeweler."

22.

That jewel in fine gems thereupon
Lifted her face, with eyes of gray;
Her crown of orient pearls put on,
And then I heard her gravely say:
"Sir, in your tale you're quite mistaken
To think your pearl is lost for eternity,
When it is comfortably not forsaken
260 In this gracious garden's tranquility,
Forever to linger and play in this place,
Where loss or mourning never appear:
It would be a splendid jewel-case,
If you were a gracious jeweler.

23.

"But, gracious jeweler, if you should lose
Your joy for a gem that was dear to you,
I think it's a maddened course you choose,
Pursuing a matter so slight to do;
For all you lost was a rose, at best,

270   That flowered and failed in nature's way;
Now, though, you see it held close in a chest
That proves it to be a pearl beyond pay.
And you have called your Fate a thief,
Which made you a man *ab nihilo;*
For your malady, you blame the relief;
Are you a grateful jeweler? No."

24.

A jewel to me then was this guest,
And noble jewels, what she had to say.
"Indeed," I said, "my loveliest,
280 You drive my great distress away.
I beg to be excused my guilt.
I thought my pearl removed for good;
Now I have found it, I shall exult,
And live with it in the shining wood,
And love my Lord, and the laws He gave,
Who has brought this blessing to me so near.
Now, were I beside you beyond this wave,
I would be a joyful jeweler."

25.

"Jeweler," replied that gem so bright,
290   "How you men jest! You're out of your mind!
Three statements you have made outright:
All three are ill-advised, you'll find.
You don't know what in the world you mean;
Wild words your wits cannot restrain.
In this dale you believe I am to be seen
Because with your eyes you see me plain;
For another, you say, in this land you dream
You shall dwell alongside me right here;
And third, that you'll cross this noble stream—
300   Which may not be done by a jeweler.

VI

26.

"I hold that jeweler deserves small praise
Who only grants what he sees with his eye,
And is much to blame for discourteous ways
Believing our Lord would tell a lie,
Who faithfully promised your soul to raise,
Though Fortune caused your flesh to die.
You dump His promises every which way
If you grant only what your eyes can spy.
And that is a point of pridefulness,
310   Which is unbefitting in any good man,
To think no other can truly assess
As well as his own judgment can.

27.

"Judge now yourself: Have you conversed
With God in a style of proper submission?
You say you shall dwell in this realm. Well, first,
I think you should ask Him for His permission—
And indeed your appeal might very well fail.
You wish to pass over this waterway:
Another counsel must first prevail.

320 Your corpse must sink into colder clay;
For it, in the groves of Paradise,
Was marred and misused by our forefather.
Each man must pay Death's cruel price
Before God allows him to cross this water."

28.

"If you condemn me, my sweet," I said,
"To sorrow again, I will pine and sigh.
Now I've found alive what I thought was dead,
Shall I lose it again before I die?
Why must I find it, but not to keep?
330   My precious pearl gives me great pain.
What can treasure do but make men weep,
If, later, it's painfully lost again?
Now I don't care if my fortunes fall,
Nor how far from the fold men drive me away.
When I am deprived of my pearl, what shall
I expect but grief to my dying day?"

29.

"You judge of nothing but deep distress,"
That young woman said. "Why do you so?
By loudly bewailing a loss that is less,
340 Men often lose sight of the greater woe.
You should, instead, make the sign of the Cross,
And love God always, be you blessed or reviled,
For anger won't win you a watercress.
Whoever must suffer should not run wild.
Though you dance about like a wounded doe,
Thrash and bellow fierce agonies,
Once you can move neither to nor fro,
You must abide what He decrees.

30.

"Though you censure the Lord, forever indict,

350   He won't veer a foot from the path He's taken.

Your returns won't increase by even a mite,

Although your sorrows are never forsaken.

Cut short your wrangling, curtail your complaint,

And beg for His mercy both fast and earnest;

Your prayer may persuade Him to practice restraint,

So Mercy can show her power at its best.

His comfort may soften the suffering you feel

And banish your pains to set you free.

You may rage or lament, mourn aloud or conceal,

360   All lies in Him to command or decree."

VII

31.

Thus I replied to that damoiselle:
"I pray my Lord will not take offense
If I wildly rave and do not speak well.
My bereavement has filled my heart with torments
Like water surging out of a spring.
I give myself up to His mercy always.
Never rebuke me with words that sting,
My precious dear, though I go astray.
Show me your comfort in every weather,
370   Piteously, and ponder this:
You who brought sorrow and me together,
Had once been the grounds of all my bliss.

32.

"You have been to me both bliss and bane,
But much the stronger was my moan:
After you were delivered from earthly pain,
I never knew where my pearl had gone.
Now I see where she is, my pain is eased.
When last we parted we were at one;
God forbid we now should be displeased,
380   We meet so seldom by stump or stone.
Though courteously you speak to me,
I am but dirt, my manners amiss:
But Mary and John, and Christ's great Mercy—
These are the grounds of my hoped-for bliss.

33.

"I see you happily blended with bliss,
And I am a man so mournful and sad:
And you pay so little attention to this,
Though the burning sorrow drives me mad.
But now I am here and you are present,
390   I would beseech you, without debate,
That you would tell me, in sober assent,
What life you have led, both early and late,
For I am happy your situation
Is worthy of worship and good, since it is
The highway for all my jubilation,
The very ground of all my bliss."

34.

"Now may bliss be your good fortune, Sir,"
Lovely of limb and face, said she,
"Here you are welcome to linger and stir,

400   For now your speech is pleasing to me.
An arrogant mood and haughty pride,
I assure you, are hotly hated here.
It gives my Lord no pleasure to chide,
For all are gentle who dwell with Him near.
And when to His dwelling place you are called,
Be deeply devout in holy meekness.
Such demeanor my Lord the Lamb will applaud,
Who is the ground of all my bliss.

35.

      "A blissful life you say I lead:

410   You would like to know its every stage.

      You're aware, when your pearl rolled into the weed,

      I was very young, of a tender age;

      But through His godhead my Lord the Lamb

      Lifted me up to marry Him,

      Crowned me as queen in bliss to bloom

      In length of days *[that shall never grow dim]*,[7]

      And have legal share in the heritage

      Of His life. So I am wholly His:

      His acclaim, His honor, His lineage,

420   Are root and ground of all my bliss."

---

7. My translation is a guess, since scholars are uncertain what this clause means.

VIII

36.

"Blissful," I said, "can this be true?—
Don't be cross if I'm not circumspect—
Are you the Queen of Heavenly blue
To whose honor this world must pay respect?
We believe in Mary, from whom Grace grew,
Who bore a child from her virgin flower;
But who might remove the crown from her—who?—
Unless she surpassed her in some power?
Now, since her sweetness is all her own,
430   We call her the Phoenix of Araby,
Which had, from its Fashioner, flawless, flown,
Just like the Queen of Courtesy."

37.

"Courteous Queen," that fair one prayed,
Kneeling, then turning up her face,
"Matchless Mother, most beautiful Maid,
Blessed beginning of every grace!"
Then she rose up, and made a pause
And spoke toward me across that space:
"Sir, many here strive for rewards and applause,
440   But none will usurp another's place:
That Empress holds all the Heavens' spirit,
And earth's, and hell's, they are hers to possess,
Yet she will drive no one from what they inherit,
For she is the Queen of Courteousness.

38.

"In the court of the Kingdom of God alive
All have properties special to them:
Each of the people when they arrive
Is made queen or king of all the realm,
Yet none deposes another, for
450   Each one is glad for what others receive
And wishes their crowns were five times more,
If that were possible to achieve.
But my Lady, who bore as a baby, Jesus,
Her dominion above us is measureless,
And that makes none of our company jealous,
For she is the Queen of Courteousness.

39.

"From Courteousness, so says Saint Paul,
We all are members of Jesus Christ:
As head, arm, leg, and navel are all
460   Faithfully to their body spliced,
So every Christian soul is in thrall
As a limb that belongs to the might of Him.
Consider: what bitterness or gall
Is attached or tied from limb to limb?
Your head feels neither envy nor spite
If your arm or finger should wear a ring.
So we respond with love and delight
Out of courtesy to each queen and king."

40.

"Courteousness," I said, "I can sense,
470 And great charity, exist among you.
But I say—may you take it without offense—
[Line missing in the original manuscript]
You are ranking yourself too high in Heaven,
If you call yourself queen, who died so young.
How much more honor must one be given
Who has endured in the world, stayed strong,
And all his long life in penance lived,
Whose bodily sufferings earn him bliss?
What greater honor might be his gift
480 Than to be crowned king by courteousness?

IX

41.

"Such courtesy is too free in its deeds,
If it's really true, what you now say.
You lived not two years on earth. Your needs
Never taught you to please God, or to pray
Either Paternoster or Creed—it's odd
To be crowned as queen on your very first day!
I can't believe it, I swear to God,
That He would turn off in so wrong a way.
Young lady, you would, in my estimation
490 Be granted in Heaven a countess' estate,
Or even a lady's of lesser station—
But a queen! That claim is ahead of date."

42.

"There is no dating the good He does,"
That worthy young woman replied. "It's true
That Truth is in all His words, because
There's nothing not right that He can do.
As Matthew tells you in your Mass,
In the gospel truth of God's full might,
In parable He made clear as glass,
500 And likened it to heavenly light.
'My realm on high is like a lord,'
He said, 'who nourishes his vines;
The passing seasons lead toward
The time to labor for the wines.

"'That time of year, the laborers knew.
Early one day the lord arose
To hire workmen for his crew,
And found some suitable, whom he chose.
They soon agreed to what he was paying—
510   A penny a day—and set off to begin
To wrestle and toil, and take great pains,
Cutting and tying, and fencing in.
The lord, as the third hour of day passed by,
Went to the market, where idle men stood.
"'You stand there idle?' he asked them. 'Why?
You think this day is gone for good?'

44.

"'We came here before this day had begun,'
All said the same in answering,
'We've been standing here since sunrise, and none—
520   No one has asked us to do a thing.'
'Go into my vineyard, do what you can,'
So said the lord, and made it clear,
'Whatever wages are due each man
By nightfall I'll pay to him, I swear.'
They went to the vines and worked on them hard,
And all day the lord went on his way,
And brought new workers to his vineyard:
Until well nigh the end of the day.

"At the time of day for evensong,

530   One hour before the sun goes down,

He saw men idle who all were strong,

And spoke to them with a sober frown,

'Why stand there idle the whole day through?'

They said they could find no pay anywhere.

'Go to my vineyard, young yeomen, do

Whatever you can that needs doing there.'

Soon the world turned brown with the end of day,

The sun went down, and it waxed late.

He summoned them all to take their pay;

540   The day had already passed its date.

X

46.

"Since the lord knew that the day was done,
He told his reeve, 'Sir, pay all that they're owed;
Give them their wages, every one,
And further, so none can reproach me as shrewd,
Line them all up in a single row,
And give every one alike a penny.
Begin with the last, who stands below,
Until you reach those who were first of the many.'
At that the firstcomers had to complain,
550 And said they had labored until they were sore,
'For only an hour these have felt the strain:
We think that we ought to take away more.

47.

"'Much longer service, we think, has been ours,
Who have suffered through the heat of the day,
Than these, who worked not even two hours,
Yet you mark them down for equal pay.'
Then said the lord to one of those, 'So,
Friend, I will not cut back on any
Of what's yours. Take it away, and go.
560   When I hired you, we agreed on a penny,
Why do you suffer a fit of pique?
Was not a penny the contract we swore?
More than the contract you cannot seek;
Why then should you be asking for more?

48.

"'What's more, how is it unlawful if I
Give a gift, or do what I like with my own?
Or is it that you have an evil eye
Because I am good and defraud no one?'
'Thus I,' said Christ, 'shall make this shift:
570   The last shall be first across the line,
And the first the last, be he never so swift,
For many are called, but few are mine.'
The poor men receive their share, although
They did arrive late and were every way poor.
Though their labor slides off with little to show,
The mercy of God is that much the more.

49.

"I have more of joy and bliss herein,
Of noble rank and a life in full bloom,
Than all the folk in the world might win

580   Demanding strict justice as their doom.
Although I'd only begun just now—
At eventide into the vineyard I'd come—
My Lord brought my wages and kept his vow:
I was paid at once the allotted sum.
Yet there were others who'd spent more time,
Who'd toiled and sweated much longer before,
And they received nothing for having been prime,
And perhaps they won't for many years more."

50.

Then I spoke further and made myself plain:
590   "I think that your story's unreasonable;
God's justice is ready and forever will reign,
Or else Holy Writ is only a fable.
In the Psalter a verse quite open to see
Makes a clear explanation, conclusively stating,
'Thou requitest each one deservedly,
As High King, always adjudicating.'
Now he that stood steadfast all day, we learn,
Gets payment later; you are paid before,
So the less you work, the more you earn,
600   And however much the less, the more."

XI

51.

"In the Kingdom of God," that gentle one said,
"There's no risk of more or less, as such,
Each worker is always equally paid,
Whether his standing is little or much.
For the generous Chieftain is never found skimping,
Whatever He deals, whether easy or hard,
He pours out his gifts like water unstinting,
Or streams from the deep whose surge never veered.
His bounty is large for whoever's impelled
610   To surrender to Him through whom sin can be sloughed.
From them no bliss will be withheld,
For the grace of God is boundless enough.

52.

"But now you will argue, and seek to checkmate,
That I have been wrong to accept here my penny,
You'll say that I who arrived so late
Am not worthy so great a payment, if any.
Did you ever hear talk of men able to stay
Always so holy in all of their prayers,
That they never forfeited, in any way,
620   The reward of the heavens that ought to be theirs?
And always more often, the older the men,
They left the smooth path and took to the rough.
Mercy and grace must steer them then,
For the grace of God is abundant enough.

53.

"The innocent have all the grace they want:
As soon as they're born, they begin their descent
Through the water of the baptismal font.
Then into the vineyard they are sent;
Soon, as the day is inlaid with dark,
630   It declines to the night of death from its birth.
Those who had died without one black mark
The gracious Lord pays his workers their worth.
They were in their places; they did his behest;
Why should He not credit their work at its price—
Yes, pay them in full, and ahead of the rest?
For the grace of God will forever suffice.

54.

"It's well known that God had, in general,
Created mankind to live in bliss;
But our first father forfeited all,
640   Through an apple he bit upon; from this
We were condemned, due to that meal,
To die in sorrow, deprived of delight,
And afterward thrust in the heat of Hell
To dwell there forever, without respite.
But for that at once came a remedy,
Rich blood ran down the cruel cross,
And precious water for our malady:
The grace of God overflowed our loss.

55.

"Enough swelled from there, up out of that well

650 Of blood and water from the broad wound;

The blood redeemed us from the torments of Hell,

And delivered us from Death's second round;

The water is baptism, truth to tell,

That followed the spear so grimly ground;

It washes our sins away as well

With which we, through Adam, in death would have drowned.

Now there is nothing in the whole round earth

Between us and bliss but what He withdrew,

Which will be restored in a blessed rebirth,

660 Which the grace of God is sufficient to do.

XII

56.

"Grace enough, any man may have,
Who sins again, if he'd repent,
Though grief and woe he well may crave,
And bear the pain, their accompaniment.
But justice, which cannot deviate,
Will always save the innocent one;
It's a verdict God could never dictate
That the guiltless ever should be undone.
The guilty one may become contrite
670   And through God's mercy be thrust to grace;
But he that never swerved from the right,
Is saved since God is just, always.

57.

"Just so, I am certain in this case,
God saves two types—by rights, not whim:
The righteous man shall see His face,
The guiltless man shall come to Him.
In this verse, so the Psalter says:
'Lord, who shall climb Thy hill so high,
Or rest within Thy holy place?'
680   He is at no loss to make reply:
'He that has done no harm with his hands,
Who has a heart both clean and light,
Sets his foot there, and still he stands'—
The innocent always is saved by right.

"The righteous man most certainly,
He shall approach that fair domain—
Not cheating his neighbors cunningly.
He does not waste his life in vain.
The righteous Solomon plainly says
690 How he gained a wise guide to conduct him in
Who made him travel by the strait ways,
And showed him God's kingdom that he might win,
Like one saying, 'Look! How lovely that land!
It's yours, if only you are brave.'
Assuredly, you should understand,
Justly the innocent one is saved.

59.

"Of righteous men, one man implored—
In the Psalter, David, as you can see—
'Never call men to judgment, Lord,
700   For none can be justified to Thee.'
And thus, when you come before the court,
Where all of us are tried, it's true,
Plead justice, and you'll be cut short,
By this same speech I've shown you to.
But, bloody on the cross, He died,
Pierced through the palms, a doleful sight.
May He grant passage, when you are tried,
By innocence, and not by right.

60.

"Let him who can read without frustration

710   Look at the Book to understand

How Jesus walked in that ancient nation

And folk brought children to His hand:

For healing and joy He spread about,

To touch their children, they prayed to Him;

His disciples harshly bade, 'Get out!'

And shouting, they did stop many of them.

Then Jesus told them, gentle and kind:

'Make way! Let the children into my sight;

For such as these is Heaven designed.'

720   The innocent always is saved by right.

XIII

61.

"Jesus called to Him all the gentle and mild
And said no man could enter His kingdom,
Unless he came like a little child;
Or else, in that place he would never come—
Guiltless, guileless, and pure, he must be,
Without spot or stain of polluting sin:
When such ones knock at the door for entry,
Quickly men shall the gate unpin,
Where the bliss is that has never grown less,
730   Which a jeweler sought through a precious stone,
And sold all his linen and wool to possess
A pearl of great price to be his alone.

62.

"This spotless pearl that he bought was so dear—
The jeweler gave all his property—
Is like Heaven's Kingdom, bright and clear,
(So said the Father of land and sea)
For it shines spotless, purely, brightly,
An endless round, serene in mood,
And common to all who live life rightly.
740   Lo, here in the midst of my chest it stood:
My Lord the Lamb, whose blood was shed,
Set, as a token of peace, this stone.
I advise you, forsake the world gone mad,
And purchase a spotless pearl of your own."

63.

"O spotless Pearl, clad with pearls so pure,
And wearing," I said, "the pearl of great price,
Who formed for you your fair figure?
Whoever clothed you was skilled and wise;
Your beauty never came out of Nature—
750 Pygmalion never painted you thus,
Nor did learned Aristotle lecture
On the nature of properties like these;
Your color surpasses the fleur-de-lys,
Your angelic bearing so courtly and true.
Tell me, bright one, what sort of office
Could produce a pearl as spotless as you?"

64.

     "My spotless Lamb mends all for all men,"
     She said, "My belovèd Destiny
     Chose me for His bride, though our wedding then
760   Indeed had not seemed likely to be.
     But when I ascended from your dank soil,
     He called me to his benignity:
     'Come hither to Me, beloved soul,
     For there's not a stain or spot in thee.'
     He gave me power as well as beauty;
     On the dais he washed my clothes in His blood
     And crowned me pure in virginity
     And adorned me with spotless pearls where I stood."

65.

"Why, spotless bride who shines like flame,
770   Whose royalty is so rich and rife,
    What kind of creature is that Lamb
    Who takes you as his wedded wife?
    You've climbed so far over others so fair
    To lead with Him a queenly life:
    Many lovely ones with well-combed hair
    Have striven for Christ through desperate strife—
    And you drove all those splendid ones out,
    All beaten away from that marriage but you,
    And all by yourself, so strong and stout,
780   A peerless maiden and spotless, too!"

XIV

66.

"Spotless," replied that lovely queen,
"Unblemished, I am, without a blot,
And that I may say my honor has been,
But 'peerless Queen'—that, I may not.
For we, the wives of the Lamb in bliss,
Are a hundred and forty-four thousand—a troop,
As is seen in the Apocalypse:
Saint John glimpsed all of them in a group,
On the hill of Zion, that lovely spot;
In a mystic dream the Apostle saw them,
790   Arrayed for the wedding on that hill plot,
The New City of Jerusalem.

67.

"In my speech I will tell of Jerusalem;
If you wish to know what kin He is of,
My Lord, my dearest Jewel, my Lamb,
My joy, my bliss, whom I freely love—
Isaiah did prophesy of Him thus,
Of his gracious meekness, piteously:
He was killed, though guiltless and glorious,
800   Without any charges of felony,
'Like a sheep to the slaughter yard He was led;
Or, taken in hand to be shorn, a lamb,
So He closed His mouth to whatever they said,'
When the Jews had Him judged in Jerusalem.

68.

"In Jerusalem my sweet Love was slain
And torn on the cross by ruffian louts:
Willing to bear all our sorrow and pain,
He took on Himself our bitterest doubts;
His face was flayed with the buffeting,
810   That had been so fair to look upon.
For our sin He counted Himself as nothing,
Who had not committed the slightest one;
He let Himself be beaten and bent
For us, on a crude cross stretched by them;
As meek as a lamb that made no complaint,
For us He died in Jerusalem.

69.

"In Jerusalem, Jordan, and Galilee,
As good Saint John was baptizing there,
His words with Isaiah's did agree:
820   So Jesus traveled toward him, where
This prophecy of Him John gave:
'Lo, God's Lamb is as steady as stone,
Who does away with the sins that are grave
That all this world has made its own.'
He never Himself had committed one
Yet to all of them He laid His claim.
Who can reckon His origin,
Who died for us in Jerusalem?

70.

"To Jerusalem, then, my Belovèd, my own,
830   My Lamb was taken twice as a child,
As each of these prophets wrote truly down,
For his ways and his nature were gentle and mild.
The third time as well is to the point
And fully described in Apocalypse:
Of His throne, around which sat the saints,
John the Apostle had a clear glimpse,
Opening the book whose leaves were square,
Where seven seals were attached to the rim:
At that sight everyone cowered there,
840   In Hell, and Earth, and Jerusalem.

XV

71.

"This Jerusalem Lamb had never a patch
Of any color but dazzling white
To which no taint or mark might attach,
The wool was so thick and rich and bright;
Therefore each soul that had never a stain
Is to that Lamb a worthy wife;
And though He fetch more, again and again,
Among us there's no dispute or strife,
But each one added we wish were five—
850   The more, the merrier, and God bless!
In larger numbers our love can thrive,
In honor more, and never less.

72.

"No one may lessen the bliss for us
Who bear this pearl upon our breast,
For they never think of quarrelsomeness
Who wear the spotless pearl as their crest.
Although our corpses shrivel in clay
And you keep lamenting without arrest,
We know completely what we should say:
860   Through one death all our hopes are blessed.
The Lamb makes us glad, our cares are cast,
He delights us all at every Mass;
Each one's bliss is strong, unsurpassed,
Since no one's honor is ever the less.

73.

"Lest you think my wondrous tale is false,
In Apocalypse you can read these lines:
'I saw the Lamb Himself,' John recalls,
'On the Mount of Zion, vibrant and fine,
And a hundred thousand maidens in waiting
870   And four and forty thousand more;
On all their foreheads, I found, in writing,
The names the Lamb and His Father bore.
Then I heard an outcry from Heaven, as loud
As the voices of many streams running in spate
And as thunder rolls through towering clouds,
That sound, I believe, was no less great.

74.

"'Nevertheless, through the uproar around,
And the voices ringing loud in my ear,
A new note then I heard them sound
880   That was, to listen to, lovely and dear:
As harpers harping their harps are heard,
They sang that new song full and clear;
In resonant notes, and excellent words,
The songs they took up were sweet to hear.
Directly in front of God's chair they were placed,
Beside the four beasts that do his behests,
And the elder men, so serious-faced,
Kept singing their same songs, never the less.

75.

    "'Nonetheless, no one's skill was so strong,

890   Whatever the crafts they had learned or knew,

    As to sing a single strain of that song,

    Except for the Lamb's own retinue;

    They are far from the earth, and brought along

    As first fruits which only are God's due,

    And to the gentle Lamb they belong,

    Being like Himself in aspect and hue:

    For lies or false talk of any sort

    Never touched their tongues, even in distress;

    That flawless company won't depart

900   From that spotless Master, never the less.'"

76.

"Let my thanks be never the less for it,"
I said, "my pearl, though I pose you a question.
I should not rudely test your wit,
Who was for Christ's bridal Chamber chosen.
A mulch of filth and dust I seem,
And you are so rich and splendid a rose
And dwell on the bank of this blissful stream,
Where life's delights may never close.
Now, lady, in whom only truth is present,
910   I would expressly ask you this,
And though I am blunderful as a peasant,
Let my prayer prevail with you, nonetheless.

XVI

77.

"Nonetheless, dear one, I beg you now,
If you can grant that this be done,
And as you are glorious without flaw,
Do not deny me this rueful boon.
Have you not lived within castle walls,
In a manor where you all dwell and meet?
You speak of Jerusalem rich and royal,
920   Where David founded his kingly seat,
But among these trees it could not sit,
That grand pile, but in Judea. And you,
Since you are spotless, immaculate,
Your dwelling place should be spotless, too.

78.

"This spotless troop you are speaking about,
A throng of thousands, your company;
They would require, without a doubt,
An enormous city, you are so many.
Such beautiful jewels in lovely ranks,
930   It would be wrong to lodge out of doors,
But here where I take my stroll by these banks,
I see no building that could be yours.
I believe you may only wander along
To look at this glorious stream for pleasure.
If you have more buildings, stout and strong,
Now teach me the way to that spot you treasure."

79.

"That spot you mean in Judea's land,"
That special being then said to me,
"That city was sought out by the Lamb
940   To suffer for mankind sorrowfully—
The Old Jerusalem, I mean;
There ended the original sin.
But the New, sent down by God, is seen
In Apocalypse, which the Apostle takes in.
That's where the Lamb without spots of black
Has ferried that fair host, all His own,
And as His flock is without a fleck,
So His moated city is without moan.

80.

"Now let me explain these cities—the two
950   Are both called 'Jerusalem,' nonetheless:
Names which mean nothing other to you
Than 'City of God' or 'Vision of Peace.'
In the one, our Peace was instantly sealed:
There the Lamb chose to suffer His pain;
In the other, Peace is the only yield,
To be reaped forever, again and again.
That is the city toward which we press
From the time our flesh is laid to rot,
Evermore to increase the glory and bliss
960   Of that troop all of whom are without spot."

81.

"Spotless maiden, so meek and mild,"
I said then to that lovely flower,
"Bring me where you are domiciled,
And let me see your blissful bower."
The fair one said, "That, God prevents:
You may not enter into His tower,
But at my request the Lamb relents,
As the greatest favor, and grants you power
To observe that enclosure from outside,
970 Though inside you may not set a foot;
To stroll its streets, you are denied,
Unless you were pure, without a spot.

XVII

82.

"For me to unfold this spot to you,
Make your way up toward the head of this stream,
And along the opposite side, I, too,
Shall follow, up to that hilltop's brim."
Hearing that, I could no longer stay still,
But moved under boughs in lovely leaf,
Until I spied on top of that hill
980 The City, and gazed with much relief.
Lower than I, beyond the brook,
Its shafts of light outshone the sun.
In Apocalypse, its shape and look
Are described by the Apostle John.

83.

As John the Apostle saw with his eyes,
Mine viewed that City of great renown:
Jerusalem, new and a royal prize,
As from Heaven it was lowered down.
The borough was all of gold, burnt bright,
990   And burnished to shine like gleaming glass,
Superb gems underneath laid tight.
Its twelve tiers bonded to the base,
The twelve foundations joined admirably:
Each layer was a different stone,
As in the Apocalypse splendidly
This town is described by Apostle John.

84.

In writing, John named every stone,
So I know these names after reading his tale.
Jasper was the bottommost one—
1000   So solid and stable, never to fail:
On the lowest level it glinted green;
Sapphire was holding the second row;
Then chalcedony, not a flaw to be seen,
In the third showed purely pale as snow;
Emerald the fourth, with its bright green face;
The sardonyx was the fifth stone;
The sixth was ruby. We know each place
From Apocalypse, through the Apostle John.

Furthermore, John adds chrysolite,
1010   The seventh gem in the city's foundation;
The eighth was beryl, clear and white;
The twin-hued topaz held the ninth station;
The chrysoprase adorned the tenth;
The noble jacinth the eleventh row;
The twelfth, more protective than jacinth,
Was the amethyst's purple-blent indigo.
Above the parapets there extends
A wall of jasper; like glass it shone.
I knew it by his descriptive comments
1020   In Apocalypse, the Apostle John.

As John described it, I saw it there:
The twelve steps were both wide and steep;
The city stood above, foursquare,
As long and broad as it was deep.
The streets of gold glittered like glass,
The wall of egg-white jasper glinting;
The dwellings within were a blazing mass
Of every type of stone they could bring.
Each square of this great mansion's frame
1030   Stretched a dozen furlongs from end to end,
Of height, of breadth, of length the same;
The Apostle observed their measurement.

XVIII

I saw even more of what John wrote down:
Each wall of that palace had three gates;
I counted twelve going all the way round.
The portals adorned with rich metal plates,
And each gate was made from a margarite,
A perfect pearl that's always bright.
On each the names were inscribed, complete,
1040 Of Israel's children, the dates kept right—
That is to say, their order of birth;
The oldest always first written thereon.
Such light gleamed, unlike the streets on earth,
That they needed neither moon nor sun.

88.

The sun and moon they could do without:
God Himself was their lantern light,
And the Lamb their lamp, I have no doubt;
Through Him all the city glistened bright.
I could see through every dwelling and wall,
1050   Their clear transparence blocked no view;
You could see the high throne there, with all
Its splendid adornments displayed for you
As John the Apostle described in his book,
Which the High God Himself was seated on;
From under the throne ran a shining brook,
Brighter than both the sun and the moon.

89.

Neither sun nor moon ever shone so sweet
As the copious stream flowing all the time;
Swiftly it rushed through every street
1060 With neither filth nor dirt nor slime.
There was no church within that city,
Neither chapel nor temple was ever built:
Its noble cathedral was the Almighty,
The Lamb that was sacrificed for our guilt.
The gates in those walls had never been closed,
But lay always open to every lane;
Since none enters there to take repose
Who under the moon bears any stain.

90.

The moon may never steal light from them;
1070   She is too spotty, her body unsightly,
And it never is night in Jerusalem:
Why should the moon climb her circuit nightly
To emulate that glorious light
That shines out from the brook's bright brim?
The planets are also too weak for the sight,
And the sun itself would be all too dim.
Around that stream the trees are freshest,
And quickly bear twelve fruits for food;
Twelve times a year they're plump for harvest,
1080   And within a month each is renewed.

91.

So great a marvel under the moon
No fleshly heart could well endure
As when I gazed on that great town,
So wondrous was its shape, and pure.
I stood as still as a dazed quail
From amazement at its fresh appearance,
And so I felt neither rest nor travail,
I was so ravished with its radiance.
For I dare to say with clear conviction,
1090   If a bodily man had borne that boon,
Though all the clerks treated his affliction,
His life would be lost beneath the moon.

XIX

92.

Just as the powerful Moon can rise
Before the day's gleam fades away,
So suddenly, in a wondrous surprise,
I saw a procession in full array.
This noble city of famous name
Was suddenly full, with no summons call,
Of identical virgins all dressed the same
1100   As my blissful one with her crown, and all
Were crowned like her in the same fashion,
Adorned in pearls and clothes of white;
On each one's breast was finely fastened
The blissful pearl, with great delight.

93.

With great delight they glided together
On golden streets that glinted like glass.
A hundred thousand I think were gathered
And their matching liveries made one mass.
Who was the gladdest would be hard to tell.
1110   The Lamb before them did proudly pass,
With seven red-gold horns visible;
Like precious pearls His clothing was.
Toward the throne they took their way;
Though many, they didn't crowd in tight,
But mild as maids gone to Mass to pray,
They all drew forward with great delight.

94.

The delight His coming brought would be
Too much to describe, it was so great:
The elders, when He approached, I could see
1120   Fell face down worshipping at His feet.
Legions of angels assembled their scattered
Sweet-smelling incense together. Then newly
Glory and glee again were uttered:
All sang to praise that splendid jewel;
The sound might strike through the earth to hell
That the Heavenly Virtues sing in their joy;
To laud the Lamb with His throngs, as well,
I conceived a great delight to join.

My delight in seeing the Lamb had raised
1130 Much wonder in me; and thus my thoughts went:
He was best and blithest, the most to be praised
On whom I had ever heard speech being spent.
So gloriously white were His clothes,
His expression modest, Himself so gentle.
But a wound both wide and wet, did show
Close to His heart; where his skin was rent,
From His white side blood gushed out in a flow.
"Alas, who did that deed?" I thought.
"Any breast ought to burn up with woe
1140 Before it took delight in that."

96.

The Lamb did not wish to diminish delight:
Although He was hurt by the wound He had,
His countenance gave no hint of His plight,
As his glances were gloriously glad.
I looked among His shining train,
Charged and laden eternally.
Then I saw my little queen again
Who I thought had stood near me in the valley.
Lord, how great the joy she displayed
1150 Among her companions, she was so white!
That sight made me resolve to wade
Out of love-longing, in my great delight.

XX

97.

Delight poured into my eye and ear;
It melted to madness my mortal mind;
When I saw my dear one, I wished to be near,
But beyond the water she was confined.
Nothing might injure me, it would seem,
To fetch me a blow and hold me down.
No one would stop me: I'd leap in that stream,
1160   And swim across it, though I might drown.
But I was shocked from that line of attack;
About to rush into the stream to my treasure,
I was blocked from that purpose and called back:
It was not to my Prince's pleasure.

98.

It did not please Him I'd made a dash
To that stream of marvels, and been so distracted;
And yet, though I'd hurried, impetuous, rash,
I was quickly restrained from the way I'd acted:
For just as I sprang to the riverbank's curb,
1170   My rashness roused me out of my dream!
I woke in that fragrant garden of herbs:
My head was laid on the mound by the stream
Where my pearl had slipped away into the ground.
I stretched myself, feeling much dismayed
And said to myself with a sighing sound,
"To that Prince's pleasure all must be paid."

99.

I was very displeased to be cast out
Abruptly from that lovely region,
From the vivid delights I saw all about;
1180 A longing struck me in a swoon of reason,
And ruefully then I began to cry,
"O Pearl," I said, "of rich renown,
What you said to me was so dear, and I
In this true vision have set it down!
For if this account is true, and you go
Thus in a brightly garlanded crown,
Then I can accept in my dungeon of woe
That you please that Prince without a frown."

100.

If I had yielded to that Prince's pleasure,
1190 And yearned for no more than was given me,
And kept myself truly to His measure,
As the pearl had prayed me to do in her plea,
Likely as not, drawn near to God's presence,
They'd have shown me more of His mysteries.
But man always hopes to grasp more of the essence,
More luck than he rightfully can seize.
Therefore my joy was destroyed totally,
Being cast from those lands that last forever.
Lord, they are mad who strive against Thee,
1200 Or offered Thee what will please Thee never.

101.

To please the Prince with what is right
Is easy enough for the Christian to do;
For I have found Him, both day and night,
A God, a Lord, and a fine Friend, too.
This happened to me as I lay on this sod,
Prostrate with grief that my pearl was gone,
Which afterward I committed to God,
In Christ's dear blessing and my own,
He in the form of bread and wine
1210   The priest shows us daily in full measure.
Lord, grant us to be humble servants of Thine,
And precious pearls unto Thine own pleasure.

Amen. Amen.

About the Translator

Photo by Muriel Ridland

J OHN Murray Ridland
was born in London
in 1933, but has
lived most of his life
in California. In 1957 he
married Muriel Thomas,
a New Zealand Fulbright
Scholar at UC Berkeley,
where he received an MA in
English in 1958. His PhD was
from the Claremont Graduate
University. Their first child,
Little John, died at six, after
a life so extraordinary that his parents felt compelled to write about
it, in *And Say What He Is: The Life of a Special Child* (MIT Press,
1975). They have two children and three grandchildren.

Dr. Ridland taught writing and literature for forty-three
years at the University of California in Santa Barbara. In 1993–
94, he was director of the University of California Education
Abroad Program in Australia. His poems have appeared in
over two hundred journals, including the *Hudson Review,* the
Atlantic, the *New Yorker, Poetry, Quadrant* (Australia), *New
Zealand Books, Hungarian Review, Able Muse,* and *Sewanee*

Review, and online with *Per Contra, Light,* and others, as well as in a dozen chapbooks.

His books of poetry include: *Fires of Home, Ode on Violence, In the Shadowless Light, Elegy for My Aunt, Palms, Life with Unkie, (Un)Extinguished Lamp/Lampara Anapagada,* and *A Brahms Card Ballad: Poems Selected for Hungarians,* issued first in Hungarian translation by the Europa Press. His latest books are *Happy in an Ordinary Thing* and *Epitome and Epiphany.* Before the present translation of *Pearl,* he translated the same poet's Middle English masterpiece, *Sir Gawain and the Green Knight,* printed in a limited letterpress edition by Juan Pascoe at Taller Martín Pescador in Michoacán, Mexico, and in an affordable edition (Able Muse Press, 2016). *Per Contra* devoted most of its issue 31 to his work, and *Askew* produced a special issue containing his two-thousand-line epic in honor of Abraham Lincoln, *A. Lincolniad.* His literary and other papers are collected in the Special Collections Library at UCSB.

On his own he translated a nineteenth-century Hungarian masterpiece by Sándor Petöfi, *John the Valiant,* first published by Corvina Press in Budapest in 1999, and later in a trilingual edition from the Dévi Foundation in Pécs and a bilingual edition from Hesperus Press in London. For his contribution to the awareness of Hungarian literature abroad, in 2009 he was presented the Balassi Sword Award. With Dr. Peter Czipott he has translated selections of poems by Miklós Radnóti, *All That Still Matters at All* (New American Press, 2014), Sándor Márai, *The Withered World* (Alma Classics, London, 2013), and Dezsö Kosztolányi, *Inebriate of Dawn.*

ALSO FROM ABLE MUSE PRESS

Jacob M. Appel, *The Cynic in Extremis – Poems*

William Baer, *Times Square and Other Stories;*
New Jersey Noir – A Novel

Lee Harlin Bahan, *A Year of Mourning (Petrarch) – Translation*

Melissa Balmain, *Walking in on People (Able Muse Book Award for Poetry)*

Ben Berman, *Strange Borderlands – Poems;*
Figuring in the Figure – Poems

Lorna Knowles Blake, *Green Hill (Able Muse Book Award for Poetry)*

Michael Cantor, *Life in the Second Circle – Poems*

Catherine Chandler, *Lines of Flight – Poems*

William Conelly, *Uncontested Grounds – Poems*

Maryann Corbett, *Credo for the Checkout Line in Winter – Poems;*
Street View – Poems

John Philip Drury, *Sea Level Rising – Poems*

Rhina P. Espaillat, *And after All – Poems*

Anna M. Evans, *Under Dark Waters: Surviving the* Titanic *– Poems*

D. R. Goodman, *Greed: A Confession – Poems*

Margaret Ann Griffiths, *Grasshopper – The Poetry of M A Griffiths*

Katie Hartsock, *Bed of Impatiens – Poems*

Elise Hempel, *Second Rain – Poems*

Jan D. Hodge, *Taking Shape – carmina figurata;*
The Bard & Scheherazade Keep Company – Poems

Ellen Kaufman, *House Music – Poems*

Carol Light, *Heaven from Steam – Poems*

Kate Light, *Character Shoes – Poems*

April Lindner, *This Bed Our Bodies Shaped – Poems*

Martin McGovern, *Bad Fame – Poems*

Jeredith Merrin, *Cup – Poems*

Richard Moore, *Selected Poems;*
         Selected Essays

Richard Newman, *All the Wasted Beauty of the World* – *Poems*

Alfred Nicol, *Animal Psalms* – *Poems*

Frank Osen, *Virtue, Big as Sin* (*Able Muse Book Award for Poetry*)

Alexander Pepple (Editor), *Able Muse Anthology;*
        Able Muse – *a review of poetry, prose & art*
        (semiannual, winter 2010 on)

James Pollock, *Sailing to Babylon* – *Poems*

Aaron Poochigian, *The Cosmic Purr* – *Poems;*
        Manhattanite (*Able Muse Book Award for Poetry*)

Jennifer Reeser, *Indigenous* – *Poems*

John Ridland, *Sir Gawain and the Green Knight* (*Anonymous*) – *Translation*

Stephen Scaer, *Pumpkin Chucking* – *Poems*

Hollis Seamon, *Corporeality* – *Stories*

Ed Shacklee, *The Blind Loon: A Bestiary*

Carrie Shipers, *Cause for Concern* (*Able Muse Book Award for Poetry*)

Matthew Buckley Smith, *Dirge for an Imaginary World*
        (*Able Muse Book Award for Poetry*)

Barbara Ellen Sorensen, *Compositions of the Dead Playing Flutes* – *Poems*

Rosemerry Wahtola Trommer, *Naked for Tea* – *Poems*

Wendy Videlock, *Slingshots and Love Plums* – *Poems;*
        The Dark Gnu and Other Poems;
        Nevertheless – *Poems*

Richard Wakefield, *A Vertical Mile* – *Poems*

Gail White, *Asperity Street* – *Poems*

Chelsea Woodard, *Vellum* – *Poems*

www.ablemusepress.com